D1365075

A DOLLAR AND A

DREAM

How an immigrant family from India came to

America and turned a dream into reality

by

S. Patel

Preface

A dollar and a dream, well, more like 78 cents. I'll tell you about that later. This book is a short story about my parents dare to dream and how they turned a dream into a reality. My parents are my heroes', my rock, my motivation and my entire world. They are not perfect, as no humans are but this book will showcase their will to succeed and the trials and tribulations of their life. I believe it is worth sharing and if it impacts one person, then I have succeeded. I will outline their childhood and upbringing in the first few chapters then, their marriage, followed by their move to America. Along the way, I will share their secrets of success in raising a successful family.

This book is dedicated to my parents without them I would not be the man I am today. I would also like to thank my family and friends thank you for being an inspiration to me and being such wonderful role models. People are greatest inspirations and all of you have shaped my life.

Along with writing this short story, I have been energized by starting a foundation, Foundation for Random Acts of Kindness. The foundation is designed for a way to give back with a variety of purposes. Start a college savings account for a youth, help with an electric bill, and show people how to be self-sufficient these; are some of the ways this foundation will give back. Thank you to my nieces and nephews for all technical aspects. Any proceeds from this book, will be donated to the foundation, so tell your family and friends to buy the book!

Table of Contents

Lioness..5

Lion..9

Marriage..11

Miracle..14

Money..17

Italiano..21

Sisters..24

Family..27

Values..30

Education..33

Religion..37

Mami..41

Sponsorships..44

Senior..47

In-Law..50

College..53

Business………………………………………………56

Niece…………………………………………………..59

Whirlwind……………………………………………..62

Atlanta…………………………………………………65

India………………...…………………………………69

Regrets………….….…………………………………72

Finance……………..…………………………………75

Choices………………..………………………………78

Assimilate…..………….………...…………………...80

Conclusion…………….………………………………83

My Mother

Lioness

Let me first begin by telling you the story of my mother.
My mom was born in Nairobi, Kenya in the late 30's. Her
family included her mother, father, two brothers and one
sister. As with every Indian family she had a hoard of
Uncles and Aunts. From the stories my mother tells me, life
in Kenya was good but painful. She lost her father at a very
young age. So many people have lost their parents at an
early age and I cannot fathom how someone makes it
through that situation. Now, her mother was left alone to
raise four kids by herself. Of course, she had some help
along the way but no matter what you have to be a strong
woman to do it. Quickly in life, my mother learned about
strength, moving forward, pride, and self-reliance.

My grandmother, from what I was told, was a Saint. She
loved everyone, she helped everyone and she provided for

her children no matter what. She gave them a roof and food every day. My mother must have learned some valuable life lessons from her. Those lessons are passed down from generation to generation. As life proceeded in Kenya, tragedy struck again, my mother's older brother committed suicide. Suicide is not common in the Indian culture, so it was difficult to handle. Again, my grandmother remained strong and fought her way to keep the family together. At this point, she must have wondered why her, but there is always a plan, you just don't always see it. As life was proceeding, they had more harsh news, my mother's little sister was very ill. They did all they could do but she didn't make it. The pain can you imagine it? How is someone able to deal with so much pain? Losing a father, an older brother and now a little sister, I could not even begin to see how I would handle it. Sometimes before I go to bed, I think about what it would be like if I was in my mother's shoes. First, I could not imagine losing my father. I would probably not have the blessed life I do now. Then, to lose an older sibling, followed by a younger sibling, I would be questioning God every day. My mother hides her pain well;

she never used it as an excuse to fail. She never used it to mask her faults. She is a fighter, a warrior, a strong woman. These life events helped her in the future and shaped her life ahead.

My grandmother decided to leave Kenya and move to India. She had an uncle there to help her get back on her feet. They needed a fresh start, a new beginning, and to somehow leave the pain behind. As my mother recollects, life in India was good, she just had her little brother and her mom. My grandmother loved helping people almost to a fault. The community in India embraced her well. Soon as time went by, my mother was at the age to get married. Now, people always say things happen for a reason, but if they had not left Kenya, my mother would not have married my father.

My Father

Lion

Pops! He was born in 1936, in India. Now, remember, even though this is not too long ago, India was ruled by the British Empire. Can you imagine living in a country where another country told you how to live? Told you what to do? Took away your freedom? Now imagine being a ten year old boy, growing up with this hatred in your heart. Fortunately, my dad has a jovial heart to counteract the rage that is in him. Just like a lion, he is prideful, strong, and determined, but has a rage that can strike at any moment. I never knew why my dad had anger issues but now reflecting on his childhood, I can see why. My father is the oldest of seven children and his story is a bit complicated but it made him who he is today. Middle class would best describe my father's upbringing. He told me his early childhood was very pleasant and being part of a big family was a blessing. My grandfather lived in a nice home in western India. From what I'm told he was a very caring, hardworking man that enjoyed life. He fathered five children and then tragedy struck. He lost his wife, my grandmother, to an illness. I never knew my grandmother; I just have one picture of her. My dad, being the oldest had to step up at a young age to help with the household. Again, losing your mother at such a young age had to be heartbreaking. I don't know how people deal with it but the pain is always with him, even today.

Grandfather still had to raise his children, had to give them a better life, so he sent my father to school. In the meantime, he remarried, and had two more children. Dad went to school to become a pharmacist and the time to get married was approaching. The way they lived back then was when someone earned money, they gave it to the household. Anything my father earned went straight to my grandfather to pay for bills, food, clothes, etc. In India they lived in what is called a joint family. Joint family is a type of extended family, which consists of parents, their children, spouses of the children and their offspring in one household. What? Can you see that happening here? Maybe we have family in the same city but not all in one house. My father and mother met through an arranged marriage. Not quite going into it blindly, but it is something that is not common here at all. The saying is in India you get married and fall in love, In America; you fall in love and get married. The household was getting chaotic, seven children, from all ages doing their own thing. Grandfather wanted to marry my dad off to bring some help in with household activities. This is when the Lion meets the Lioness. Two prideful, determined, heavy hearted people come together.

Fifty Eight Years still married

Marriage

Indian marriages are like festivals, big all day affairs, filled with all types of emotion. My parents got married in 1962; my dad actually was not the first in the family to get married. His sister ran away from home and got married without my grandparent's approval. She was not spoken of for a very long time. So now my mom came into a joint family with my father, grandparents, and five of my dad's siblings. This was not the pride she imagined as a child but was forced into, for now. It was just the way it was back then. She was delegated to do all the daily chores of a large household. It was definitely rough for her, but a few years after marriage a blessing or two came. My parents had twin girls, my sisters. Without them knowing, they kind of changed the dynamics in the house. Children always do.

Now, as my parents were starting a family, my uncle got married. Guess what? My aunt was bought in the joint family. Now my mom had a partner in crime. She told me hilarious stories of both them, and I am glad they had each other. My aunt and uncle soon had a son, and the joint family was growing. My other uncle got married and moved his wife in the household. By the late sixties the house was packed. My grandparents, my parents, my sisters, and a cousin brother all occupied the house. In a nearby town, my mother's brother got married and had a boy. Life must have been hectic, as a matter a fact, too hectic. Too many personalities, egos, and tight living quarters, made my parents think more about their future. Is this where they want to raise a family? Can they break the cycle of working class citizens? Do they want their own home? My father made a decision. Why not apply for a green card to the United States? It would be like hitting the lottery, but if he did get a green card, he could change his family's destiny forever. 1970 was here and boom, 2 miracles!

My Sisters

Miracle

I wish everyone from the United States would travel to a third world country to see how people, live, see their daily lifestyle, and see what values they were raised on. I feel like people take our country for granted. Miracle one, my father hits the green card lottery. Millions of people apply to come to the United States every year from all over the world. India is the second most populated country on this planet, so the odds are even harder. My dad had a little advantage; he studied to be a pharmacist, so that gave him some leverage in his green card application. Now, comes the hard part, to tell his dad, he will be leaving the joint family to make his own destiny.

78 cents! 78 cents back in 1969 was still was not much money. 78 cents is what my grandfather gave my father to come to the United States. Grandfather did not want my dad to leave the joint family. He was against the idea of leaving your family to go to a foreign land, so my dad had

to sell any valuable possession he had, from music equipment to his bicycle to scrape up enough money to get a plane ticket to the United States. His cousin brother was already there and had an apartment my dad could stay in. So my dad took the 78 cents and whatever he could gather and left for America. Chasing a dream!

Miracle number two, my mother is pregnant. My father did not want any more children and he definitely did he did not want another girl. He was against the idea of trying for a boy but mom won! Their twin daughters are five years old, just startling school and now another child is the way. My mother was due in June but Dad leaves for America in May. Mom decided to go live with her mother during the pregnancy. My grandmother wanted a boy, and just thought it was a blessing to have girls before a boy. My father was afraid it would be a girl and that he would not be able afford any more children. Either way, too late, I was coming to this world!

Father arrived in the United States in May and stayed in an apartment with his cousin brother and six other guys. Mom just gave birth to her son in June. I never asked my dad if he regretted not seeing his son being born but from a selfish standpoint, I am happy with the decision he made. My dad found a job and now he was in savings mode.

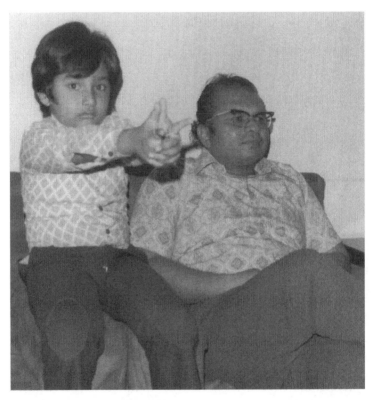

Me and my Father...check you the style!

Money

Growing up in an Indian household back in the day was nothing like it is now. I know my parents were the first generation to be in the United States and had to sacrifice on so many things but looking back at it, it's kind of funny. So my father saved enough money to get an apartment on his own in Hoboken, New Jersey. In India, my mother was going through daily struggles with her joint family. She was in a helpless situation with two daughters and a son but without her husband. Finally, the green card for me and my mom was approved and my dad saved enough to send a one way ticket to the States. Its 1972, America was still young, war, racial injustice, and stalled economy. Sound familiar? My sisters were left behind and were enrolled in an English speaking boarding school. It must have been heart breaking for them and my parents but financially my parents could not afford to bring them right now.

My parents were in full savings mode. We moved to Jersey City in a better area which was my second move. My parents had plans to buy a house and then bring my sisters over. Savings mode was doing anything and everything they could to make a penny. Dad had a full time job at a pharmaceutical company and my mom started a babysitting gig at the apartment. Dad would do side jobs after work and mom tried to recruit as many kids as she could. After three years of saving, and some borrowed money, they bought a small quaint house in Leonia, New Jersey.

Leonia was an upgrade, a neighborhood filled with families and a great school system. At this time I was around five years and was able to go kindergarten. Savings mode was not over, it was just beginning.

I remember as a kid, I would wear the same clothes every three days. All my friends would get bicycles, clothes, games and toys. I was left with my imagination. Don't get me wrong, my parents bought a few things here and there but they were trying to save everything. Looking back, I was actually very thankful I didn't get everything. It helped spur my brain by being able to imagine or dream. I would create games or play out scenarios, and share them with the neighborhood kids. It taught me so much, instead of having things just handed to me. That's when I started my first business, which was a gutter cleaning service. Me and two friends of mine would go around the neighborhood cleaning gutters or do any work the customer wanted. Soon after, I got my own newspaper route. Now, as a typical kid I would spend money on candy, toys, or a new football but I learned from my parents. I opened a savings account and would deposit my money there weekly. My father's life lesson: pay yourself first. He taught me that from every single paycheck I get, deposit a percentage into a savings account and don't touch that money. A lesson I still use to this day.

My parents hated to borrow money but had to do so in order to get our house. Their main goal was to payback any debt and start saving. My mother must have started couponing. Everything we got was from a sale or bargain.

My sneakers came from a grocery store, crazy to think that now. I asked my parents later on if we were on food stamps. My father said he knew it was available, and he knew they were eligible, but for him personally, it would bring shame to his household. He took it as a personal insult and thought if he accepted welfare it meant he could not provide for his family. I remember he told me, "I did not come to America for free food, free housing or free anything; I came here to fulfill a dream. Free anything was not in my dreams, only hard work. We did not take free things but we did accept help."

Me, Mom and Dad….look Twin Towers!

Italiano

For some reason, I still have vivid memories of going to school. My parents spoke Gujarti - a dialect of Hindi - and did not really teach me English. I have a memory of kids in class making fun of me because every time I spoke it was in Gujarti. I did not know any better but it is surprising, how at a young age, you can pick things up so quickly. So my parents after work would help me with English lessons. Typical Indian parents, as they were, they spent twenty percent of the time on English and eighty percent of the time on Math. My parents were dedicated to succeed and they had multiple jobs at this point. Dad would get up early, go to work and then do a side job, and go home in the late evening. Mom, at one point had three jobs. She worked at a book company, a toy company and anywhere else she could do to make money. I was walking to school in the mornings and when I came home, I would have to stay at my neighbor's house, until one of my parents got home.

My neighbors were these two elderly Italian ladies, with hearts of gold.

For the life of me, I cannot remember their names but they gave me mine. Sambino! We were Indian immigrants that did not speak much English and they were Italian immigrants that did not speak much English. What a combination! How you doing? Kem Cho? We all in knew one word though, Pizza! These two ladies would keep me after school, feed me, help with homework and let me play outside. They were awesome! You almost cannot, or do not, do that now a days, it's unheard of. As a few years went by, my parents gave me a key to the house, and I would take care of myself. Of course, some days, I came close to burning the house down, or threw the key chain in the tree, or lost the keys in my snow fort. Hey, it happens.

The world changes fast but some things should not change. Neighborhoods are not the same; schools are not the same, family values are not the same, education is not the same, but one thing remains a constant; money. The days of it takes villages to raise a child are diminishing. It's a sad day but you have to adapt.

Life was good; I remember my dad taught me multiplication by the age of six. I picked up English fast and taught it to my parents. I used to get the highest grades in school for Math. We had a roof over our heads, food on the table, friends to play with, and family close by to visit. I was a top of the world. I got all the attention, played till dark, and had no worries in the world. I did not even know or realize I had sisters.

The Twins at school in India

Sisters

My parents would go to a friends or family member's house on Sundays for some much needed relaxation. We would play games and eat, the kids would play; it was just a great gathering of people. One Sunday, life changed forever. My dad received a call from a security guard from the airport. The guard proceeded to say that his two daughters were there crying and waiting on him to pick them up. My father was told the date and time in India and nobody caught the time difference. My twin sisters were waiting in airport by themselves and had no clue why their parents were not there. Welcome to America! What a way to arrive. Luckily they spoke some English, and someone gave them change to make a phone call. They called several times but no answer. We were at my dad's cousin brother's house. When we got home in the evening, the phone rang, and the mad rush to the airport was on. Safe!

I find many similarities between our family and a lion's family. The male lion has strength, courage, power, fierceness, rage and is the protector of his family. That's my dad; don't get him angry he just has to give you that look one time. I peed in my pants plenty of times because of the look. Since he was young, he protected his siblings and now he protects his family. The lioness has raw power, the hunter, protector, nurturing and the behind the scenes bread winner. That's my mom. Not only did she cook and clean, she worked three jobs to bring money home. Our pride grew by two and to be honest, my sisters were a blessing.

Of course, we would have normal brother sister fights or arguments but they were truly role models for me. My sisters were honest, loving, caring and smart and have many more qualities that I was fond of. We joke around that my sisters used to gang up on me and beat me with a bat but if that the only incident I can come up with, wow, we did good.

I wonder what it was like for my sisters. They had each other throughout their childhood but when their parents left them in India, it must have hurt them. First their father leaves to go to a foreign country, then two year later their mother and brother leave as well. Fortunately for them, they were surrounded by family. My Grandfather, cared for them greatly, he would visit them in boarding school and bring them candy and treats. For a year or so, Mom had to separate the two, one sister stayed at my grandfather's house and the other stayed with my mom's mother. My uncle was married by now and my aunt took care of my one sister for over a year. Now, I know why they are close. I never knew that until recently. My other sister always talked about her grandfather, it all makes sense.

So, my sisters are in America, we all are going to school, parents are working hard, and life was good. My parents paid back every loan they received from friends and started to build a nest egg. In our culture, there are five main priorities in life; family, values, education, religion and money. Even though, my parents left their immediate family, they had their own to take care of. These five priorities should be the staple in every family; this is the main difference between the culture in the United States and the culture I was raised on.

The Twins were introduced to the art of snowball fighting

Family

Number one priority in life is your family, I learned that very early. You have your inner core family- (parents and siblings), and the outer core, aunts, uncles, and cousins. The biggest difference today is that in America, family is not the top priority. I am speaking in general. You always hear, once a child is eighteen they are out of the house. My child is eighteen, I taught them what I can, and they are no longer my responsibility. Even a child's mentality is that when they turn eighteen, they cannot wait to get out of the house. They leave the house, create debt, get in trouble, ruin their credit, and just set their future to be playing catch up rather than moving ahead.

My parents gave us no choice by telling us at a young age that we were going to college. We were going to do better than them. They would pay for school, and we could stay in the house as long as we were seeking higher education or working. Family first! If you have a tight knit family, you can accomplish many goals.

So at this point, my parents, so far, have had success in America. Their children are in school, their family is healthy, and we have a secure roof over our heads. The plan now was to save for higher education and they would have some big bills coming up. The twins were in high school and college was on the horizon. I was six years behind them, so I didn't have a care in the world. My dad was working for a pharmaceutical company but could not get promoted. My mom was a star at a publishing company but was stuck in her role. It's kind of funny, in today's world, someone could cry out racism, but my parents did not see color. They were stuck in their jobs and were limited in the amount of money they could make.

My father kept in touch with his family in India and would even send my grandfather money. My uncle soon left India and started to run a hotel. His wife's brother had got into the hotel business and had an opportunity for them. My uncle kept trying to convince my dad to work for himself. Now, my dad was starting to listen. They had an opportunity to purchase a twenty-unit motel in South Carolina. They could be the masters of their own destiny or they could flop and would have to start all over again. They decided to go all in. Take a chance. If they could succeed in this, the twin's education would be a possibility.

In order to purchase this business, they needed to scrape and claw, to come up with a down payment. They had just paid back their friends for the loans for the house, so, my dad decided to partner up with my uncle to purchase this property, but he still had the majority shares. My parents even emptied my savings account to come up with enough money; they used every dollar they could get. We were on the move again, no risk no reward. Our fifth move, but this time many miles away from friends and family.

U.S. 1 in Camden, South Carolina

Values

Camden, what a beautiful place. Quiet, peaceful, and that southern hospitality thing, that's for real. My parents did it; they went from working countless jobs to being business owners. To clear a stereotype, they did not receive a minority loan or handout from the government to buy their business. They bought it with their hard earned money and help from family and friends. Do you see the common theme yet? Family first!

Now, at the hotel, my parents had to take care of everything. Fix anything that broke, clean rooms, landscape, take care of their house and even promote their business. Just having a business does not make you rich, you still needed customers and you needed to grow the business to succeed. My dad learned to be a jack of all trades and he would bring me along so I could learn. Trust me, it was no paper route, but I was learning the value of hard work - with no pay. My mom would clean rooms, manage the front desk, and take care of the house. My sisters had jobs and would also fill in at the hotel doing various jobs. They had a year or so left before they were eligible for college.

I learned so many values from being raised in South Carolina. Along with my parents influence, growing up in South Carolina, I learned about loyalty, respect, reputation, honesty, determination, challenge, and balance. I remember one day I got in trouble for stealing change from my parents. My dad sold stamps in a box as a side gig and would keep the profits in a change jar. Well, I figured it was a community jar, even though I knew better, and I would buy candy, baseball cards, and food with that money. I got caught one day and was not honest. My parents never really hit us as children but my dad made me cross my legs and touch my toes for four straight hours. He gave me that look and yes a peed in my pants. I learned about honesty that day.

Throughout my childhood, we were taught all types of values. My parents were in a foreign country and did not want to rock the boat. We encountered racism and I will talk about that later. Today, with all my lessons learned, I try to uphold to those same values but I mainly live by three. These three values - kindness, compassion, and love - have changed my life. It's pretty simple; let go of your ego, arrogance, selfishness, and life will be less stressful and more fulfilling. We are here on Earth for a short time, so we might as well enjoy it. You can always change your core values. Think of yourself like a house. If you change the windows, or paint the house, it seems new but in time it will fade away. If you tear the house down and change its foundation, it will be new. You can always change your foundation or inner core, it just takes practice and time. You must want to do it and be determined for a better life. Let that ego go!

My Sister's high school graduation…Go Bulldogs!

Education

The 80's are here, Ronald Reagan is president, the music was innovative, the computer was introduced and life was just good. We as a family didn't have much but we used our imagination and creativity to enjoy life. We still didn't have much money, my parents were trying to build a business and pay back loans. My sisters and I still had to walk to school, while kids their age had cars and kids my age had a bicycle. We were thankful that the winters were not as cold like in New Jersey.

My parents are Hindu and tried to raise us the same way but adapted to their new country. Even though Christmas was a Christian holiday, my parents assimilated, and gave us the best Christmas they could. They knew everyone in the whole country was involved and they had to be included. I think my sisters got a car right before college started and I received a bicycle. My sister's got accepted to the University of South Carolina. Back then, it did not seem a big deal but now, I am astonished. They came here from India only a few years ago and they got accepted to a huge University. One of my sisters was majoring in Nursing and the other was majoring in Computer Programming. Year by year, my parents' dream was coming to fruition. That does not mean the road was easy for any of us. Education had to be paid for; we did not qualify for financial aid or scholarships.

I was cruising through middle school; it seemed that the education system was better up north. Math, science, and social studies were a breeze. The only issue I had was making friends. See, half the kids were Caucasian and the other half were African American. I was considered an "other", at least that's the box I had to check on my forms or tests. We did not have any other Asian kids in school except me, which was good and bad. The good was that kids are curious; they thought it was cool that I ate different food, spoke a different language, and dressed differently. The bad was that, kids can be mean to people who are different than them. My parents taught me about respect, not only for them, but others too. If I showed someone respect, I should get the same in return, if not, walk away. I never got in a fight in my life.

My parents stressed our education constantly. They knew that with a proper education we would have a leg up. America gave us an opportunity, and we capitalized on it. My parents always checked our grades and pushed us to be better. I remember one day I received an award for the highest grade in history and brought that certificate home to show my dad. His reaction was not "Great job!" but rather, he wanted to know where the award for math and science was. See in the Indian culture, Math and Science are pushed; they know that they lead to good paying jobs. As a kid, I was extremely upset that my dad didn't congratulate me and threw my certificate in the garbage. As an adult, I understand where he was coming from but still do not agree with the way it was handled.

Math and science were never my strengths, I loved history and physical education. I played all sports in New Jersey, from stickball to street hockey. The problem in Carolina was we didn't live in a neighborhood, no kids around. I asked my dad for a basketball hoop one day and he pretty much put it on the back burner. My chores included, cutting the grass, sweeping the parking lot, helping my dad and studying. So in my spare time, I decided to take a used plastic plant pot, cut the bottom out and staple it to a tree. Using a ladder, I put the "hoop" about ten feet high and now I could play basketball. I would come up with my own games and do the same with a baseball and a wall. Kids need imagination in today's world. Let them be creative without giving them every resource. It did wonders for me later on in life.

Off my tangent, my sister's received their Bachelor's degrees in four years and started to pursue their careers. They did not leave the household, they contributed to it. I was off to high school. Before classes started we had to take pictures for the yearbook. Males had to wear a suit and; I never owned a suit, so I never got my picture taken.

Life was about to change again, my cousin from Germany was enrolling to study here; with me.

My Cousin Brother from Germany and me!

Religion

My parents are very religious people. They remained true to their heritage, and still do to this day. They tried to raise us as Hindus but also let us find our way. I think they knew being in America, they could not force religion on us, so they instilled core values in us instead. I believe that things happen for a reason, and believe in karma, honesty, respect, and balance. I mentioned before that my mother only had one brother left; he was living in Germany, with his wife and three kids. My grandmother moved with him to Germany and where he was a successful disc jockey. I remember they came to visit us in South Carolina and this was the first time I met my cousin brothers. My grandmother had just passed away in Germany. I still remember my mother crying on the phone when she got the news. She just had one brother left in her immediate family.

It's the little things you remember! My uncle was going to Disney World for a few days and my father and I decided to join them. What a trip! Seven people packed in a Volvo for ten hours. My father driving on the wrong side of the road in Orlando, all of us in one hotel room, astonished we made it. My uncle was awesome, so jovial, and an outstanding cook. He made this dish that I can still taste in my mouth. My mother was so happy to see him and that made me happy. I had met two other cousin brothers on my dad's side, and it was nice to meet family on my mom's side as well. The family must have talked about the possibility of moving to America because a few months later my cousin brother was going to be a junior in high school - my high school! It was a blessing. I never had a brother, someone to show me the way, teach me things or help me daily life struggles, and now I was getting one.

I was truly blessed. My cousin and I had the best time in South Carolina. He was a great role model for me. For him to leave his family to go to school in America must have been difficult. I know I did not make things easier. God gave me an older brother, I was happy. He basically showed me the way, from high school, to college, and throughout life. I observed what he did and tried to follow, but I was not the man he is.

One of the hardest days in my life was in my sophomore year in high school. I questioned god, and almost lost faith in god and religion. I remember it like it was yesterday. I was in the living room and my cousin received a call from his mother in Germany. He started yelling "No, No!" and then started crying. My mom came rushing over, she knew - my uncle had passed away. My cousin lost his father in a bout with alcoholism and my mother had lost her last sibling. I watched them both comfort each other and I had no words. What can you say? What can you do? With that said, I think I lost my religion that day. How is this possible? How can this happen? Why is god so cruel? There cannot be a god that would take a way a father from a family and leave a woman alone to take care of three growing children. I lost religion that day but as time went by I gained spiritualism.

I watched my cousin in life; he has this inner strength and determination within him. I saw him approach life with this fire, whether it was in school or on the basketball court. All three of my cousin brothers have this same spirit in them. My Aunt got sponsored by her brother in New Jersey and moved to America with my two other cousin brothers. My oldest cousin brother that was staying with us got accepted to college and my Aunt found a job in Greenville. Again, family first!

My parents showed me determination, but my cousin, taught me determination. This kid would not fail in anything. I mean anything. He played on our high school soccer team, with full blown asthma. He kicked my ass in every sport from tennis to basketball even when we were just play wrestling in the living room. He carried this determination through college and then into his work and family life. I observed and learned from him greatly.

My other Mother

Mami

My cousin graduated from high school and enrolled in college for the fall term. My Aunt found an apartment, and the boys quickly got acclimated to the American lifestyle. They all found friends very quickly and started to establish roots there. Greenville was just a perfect place for them. A great culture to raise kids, great education, employment opportunities, and a community unlike any other I have ever seen. The Indian community embraced my Aunt with open arms. I would frequently visit them and had some of my best times as a youth there. I remember playing basketball or football with my cousins and their friends. We had such great times, and I was so happy they made friends quickly.

Mami in our language means Aunt. For me, she is my second mother. Mami, taught me so many lessons in life. Every time I visited, she took care of me as if I was her own child. Her demeanor was so pleasant, that I could not see any pain in her. She raised those three boys on her own, provided a home, education, and most importantly a security blanket for them.

Determination is roughly described as that feeling that you have as you persevere towards a goal or accomplishment in spite of the obstacles in your way. Well, my Mami, was determined to give those boys everything she could. I watched her come home from work, probably tired, but then start to make dinner, clean up afterwards, make lunches for the next day and later in the evening sit down to watch a show or two. How she made time for everything she had to do to run a household, I never understood. I admired her determination so much, and if I could have half of that in me, I would be a better man.

I would visit my Mami quite often in my first year of college, as I was only an hour away. She does not know but I learned so much about life from her. I learned about being fiscally responsible. I would go grocery shopping with her and notice the products she would buy and how she used coupons. It was free money, right? Every bit helped and I think today, people just impulse buy. I would watch how she lived; she worked hard but also took the time off to enjoy life.

One of the best qualities I admired about my Mami was that she liked adventure and travel. Even to this day, she travels and has been all over the world. I used to travel and need to get back on it. She taught me the old saying; work hard and play hard.

My Mami and Mom are the strongest women I have ever met. Although they are different people, they have similar characteristics. They are the Lioness's of their pride. Men can show off their physical strength but there is no strength like the heart of a woman. Their heart has endured so much pain, anguish, agony and affliction but yet they overcame every obstacle in life. I strive to have their qualities. What terrific role models!

My Dads brothers…my Uncles

Sponsorships

I got my high school back!! My cousin brother graduated
and moved on to college. Although, I loved him dearly, he
indirectly put pressure on me. He was smart, played on the
soccer team, and was very personable. Me, I was a metal
head, loner, shy, and pudgy. Just about every teacher said,
"You are not like your sisters or cousin!' They all
remembered us because we were the only Indian people
that attended high school. So, now I am a junior in high
school and life is good. I started a side hustle. I would make
mixed tapes and sell them at school. I made enough money
to start buying music equipment and usually just stayed in
my room. Then another turn of events came back to back.

My father sponsored his sister to come to America and she
did. They came from England and with their brother from
North Carolina's help bought a small hotel in Columbia,
South Carolina. Things were moving fast. His brother and
sister were now here and close by. He only had four

siblings left in India. So far, the American success story was panning out for everyone, so they wanted to follow my father's lead. Family first!

After my Aunt settled in Columbia, my dad's brother was sponsored to come to America. Now, he would stay with us and bought my cousin brother and sister with him. This uncle, he was cool and jovial person. The fun uncle! He had a heart of gold and just wanted to enjoy life. My cousin brother and I got along well and would enjoy each other's company. He had his father's heart. Unfortunately, one of my memories of him as a youth was not a fond one. He was not the smartest kid in school but he tried. Nonetheless, his mom would beat the living daylights out of him. I remember standing there one day, she was asking questions and if he got them wrong, a beating would come. Just the mental abuse that kid went though was horrible. She kept berating him, telling him that he was stupid and that he would never amount to anything. It was hard to see, and it still hurts to think of that memory.

My uncle and his family decided to move to Chicago where he had a friend that would help him get established. Everyone in the family was getting settled and established. My father was trying different ventures to make more money. When he bought the motel it came with an ice cream and fast food shop. I believed we all worked there at one time or another. He sold that and then opened a liquor store in Columbia. You have to take risks in life in order to succeed.

Senior days in high school

Senior

My last year in high school was great and scary at the same time. Right now, I was coasting through school, I think my grade point average was just above a 2.0. I do not think my parents were even paying attention. I was really bored in high school and the only class I enjoyed was a drafting class. When I was a kid, I loved playing with LEGOs and would build houses and other structures. In my drafting class I was able to do the same, but on paper. I would layout towns, draw houses and really get in depth with designs. All the other classes were boring and it just was too hard for me to focus.

My parents were extremely busy; mom was at the hotel doing her thing, dad was between the hotel and liquor store. My sisters graduated college and were working in their fields. My mother was ready to find them grooms to marry. She insisted on going to India to find them the right person. Me, I was watching the process, scared out of my mind.

Am I going to have to go to India to get married? What the heck? My sisters were still more traditional and not fully Americanized.

As I senior I was not thinking about college…, I just knew I had to go somewhere. My sister and mom left to go to India in search of a marriage partner. I started to gain more freedom and my parents started to cut the cord with me. Word came from my mom that my sister found a husband and she was to get married in India. At the same time, my parents were looking to make a move again, this time to Florida. My father now had his sister and my brother who was previously in Chicago, in Florida. They both owned a convenience store. In a swift move, they decided to sell all their assets and buy a laundromat in Florida; Port St. John, Florida, right where the space center is. The lure of being closer to family, better climate and low taxes brought my parents to Florida. Family First!

I graduated high school but decided to stay in South Carolina for college. The rest of the family moved to Florida, including my new brother in law.

The In-Laws

In-Law

My parents rented a small house in town and I stayed there for the summer until college started. I was soon to meet my brother in law. He left his parents and brother to come to America and start his own family with my sister. Can you imagine that? Think about it...Could you leave your family and friends, get married to someone you barely know and then move to a foreign country? No Way! We all tried to make him feel welcome but as a man, that had to be tough on him. My dad got him involved in the family business and my sister was working as well. They stayed with my parents until they saved enough money to move out on their own. What a big difference in our culture versus the American culture.

My sister graduated college debt free; my parents saved money year by year to pay for it. They also let us stay at home, rent free until we could establish our own home without debt. So, my brother-in-law, recently married, was to stay in our house until it was time to move on. He had to live with his in laws, work for their business, eat their cooking, and try to be included in the family dynamics. My other sister was at the house as well and she was soon to be married. I admire my brother-in-law greatly. What a leap of faith! I learned from him as well; he taught me about courage, faith, growth, poise, success, and many other qualities. Family first!

Our family was establishing roots in Port St. John. The laundromat was tough and my father saw an opportunity to buy an empty gas station that was for sale. He jumped on it. Probably the best business decision he ever made. He included his brother in the business and hired my brother-in-law to manage it. Fall was coming and fast, and so was my first year of college.

e

Florida

College

As I stated before, education was a priority for my parents. As typical parents they wanted their children to do better than them. I decided to stay in South Carolina for my first year of college, about an hour away from my Mami and cousin brothers. My parents did not have the full funding for my education, so we had to take out a student loan. I left Florida, and I swear I cried from Port St. John to Jacksonville; it was my first time away from my family. My Mami always treated me as I was one of her own, but for this upcoming year, I was going to live on campus.

Campus life was great, I met new friends, saw some high school classmates, and enjoyed the independence. I worked at a day labor company and saved some money for miscellaneous expenses. College was much better than high school for me. I was intrigued. My grades went from a 2.0 in high school to a 3.5 in college. I was being challenged. With the core values my parents taught me, I look back and now see how I was able to succeed. The only problem was I missed being around my family, so I decided to transfer to the University of Florida.

At the University of Florida, I had some of my best years in life. I learned so much about people and life, but towards the end I started to get bored again. During holiday breaks, I would work at my dad's business. I enjoyed the business world and was intrigued with money. Leave it to me, of the five core principals of life my parents taught me - family, values, education, religion, and money, I was fascinated with the latter. After college was over, I moved back home with my parents. My sister and her husband had moved out to start their own family and my other sister was off to India to get married. She met my other brother-in-law and got married and he came to America. I admire his courage and will power to leave his family and move to a different country. I worked at my dad's c-store and wanted to learn all about business.

U.S. 1 Port St. John, Florida

Business

My father opened a closed gas station and basically made it into a beer store. He did not receive free money, government loans, or any other handout. He saved money, found a partner in my uncle and started this business from scratch. His primary focus was customer service and sell by volume. His past experience led him to know that customer service was a priority. I learned so much more from this business than I ever did in college. I learned everything from accounting to management, which would help me later on in life.

My parents have always worked hard and now they would be tested again. The store was open from 6 am to 10 pm, 7 days a week, 365 days a year. They both worked every day, all day, no holidays or weekends off. When I moved back home, I helped by working some hours. My parents did not charge me rent or have me pay bills in the household. They let me establish a little savings before I moved out on my own. Just another concept you don't see that often in America. Why burden your child with debt? When any of my parent's children moved out, we were debt free and had a strong foundation to be out on our own.

So, all is well, we are all trucking along as a family and then we received the best news ever. My sister was pregnant and would have a baby girl. My niece would be the eldest amongst her cousins and the first born in America. We all were excited and could not wait for that day. People do not realize how hard having your own business is. Somebody always missed out on an event to run the business. Somebody missed out on a trip, birthday party, dinners, holidays, or birth in the family.

The store life was very repetitive. Day in, day out, same people, same sales person; dealing with the public was no joke. I could write a book with the customer encounters I had alone. We were all determined to succeed, all in, and we all put effort into making this business successful. In the matter of a few years, we made our store the number one ranked store in beer sales for an independent account in the whole county. A tiny store in Port St. John was outselling national chain stores and even big grocery stores. I learned valuable lessons from my father through his business.

Even though we all put hours in work, we had to find a balance in life. When you're up, try bringing it down and when you're down, bring it up. Balance was very important; we all tried having dinner once a week, going to a movie, visiting the beach or doing something besides work. Balance is a key to my life today. I use balance today, in all aspects of life, from relationships to finance.

My sister and niece....best picture ever!

Niece

What a blessing it is to have a child. I do not have any children and could only imagine what parents must go through in seeing a child born and raising them to adulthood. My niece…,what can I say about her? From when she was a child, everyone knew she was destined for greatness. You know when you see a kid and you just know; man that kid is special! That's my niece. I know why parents say when they have a child they would die from them. I would die for my niece!

My niece brought joy to our household; she was that ray of sunshine. As child, she was very curious and wanted to learn. Watching her grow up has been a blessing from me. She too was instilled with determination and the will to succeed. So here is a question. Are people born with certain attributes or are they taught them? The answer is both. I believe we are born with certain talents but you also have to choose to use them. With your parent's guidance, a person chooses to take their talents and perfect them. My niece made a choice. She chose to be successful one day, and she has worked extremely hard for it. She has the coolest goal ever! She wants to be a pediatrician and deliver the first human in space. Step one is complete.

After a few years, my sister and brother-in-law decided to move to New Jersey and establish their own roots. This allowed me a bigger role in the business. My niece stayed here for a bit and then eventually moved up north. My brother is an Engineer and wanted to work in the corporate world, while my sister was in the Information Technology field. Soon, they would be blessed with another child.

My nephew...blinging

Whirlwind

So it is the mid 90's. My sister is in New Jersey and just had a baby boy. My other sister is in Florida and just had a baby girl. She is a Nurse and my brother-in-law is a Radiologist. Soon they will leave Florida for Kentucky. So, I have two beautiful nieces and a handsome nephew. Have you ever looked at a child and see a certain spirit in them? It's hard to explain but even though they are a child, you can see their inner beauty. It's almost like they have the spirit of god in them. That's my nephew. My nephew was playful, joyous, full of laughter, and a just well-mannered kid. My niece in Kentucky was too cute as a child. She should have done commercials. Soon, she welcomed in a baby brother.

Everything seemed to move so fast. Life just keeps moving on. My sister in New Jersey moved backed to Florida. They bought out my uncle shares from the store and were now equal partners with my father. My uncle was fighting with alcoholism and it just did not work out in our business. He and his family decided to move to Atlanta, and start fresh. All my cousins were grown up, some went into business with their family and some decided to work in the corporate world.

I decided to move out myself and bought a condo in town. I needed to gain independence and start to establish some credit. I used the savings I had to place a down payment and welcomed myself to debt. A good debt!

The store was humming along, nieces and nephews were getting big, everyone was doing great except for me. For some reason, I felt a void in my life. I felt that I was riding my father's coat tail. Now I knew why my brother-in-law left. There was an itch I had to scratch. So my best friend and I decided to move away from Florida. I knew the store was in good hands with my brother-in-law and my parents were still young enough to work.

My sister, brother-in-law, niece, and nephew in

Kentucky

Atlanta

One of the riskiet decisions I made in life was to move to Atlanta in 2000. So, my best friend and I decided to pack up our belongings and look for career opportunities in Atlanta. We did not have a job lined up, a place to move into, or a clue. My cousin brother, who was in Atlanta, let us stay with him for a few days, while we went apartment hunting. We found an apartment in North Atlanta and moved in over the weekend. We were in Florida on Thursday and job hunting in Atlanta on Monday. Any job would suffice right now; we needed income to pay next month's rent. Both of us did odds jobs until we found more of a career job. Life had shown me determination, hard work ethics, and the will to succeed through various role models, and now, it was my time to shine.

My first career job was working at a for profit college and enrolling new students. My initial interview went great but the hiring process stalled. See, corporate America only see's you on paper, they cannot read your determination or character. So I was low balled on my starting salary with a promise to get a review every six months. I went to training and the report my boss received was that I was probably not going to last a year. I think I was just soaking the information in, a little home sick and just questioned myself. Despite this, I was not going to fail!

The company had an awards banquet at the end of every year, this particular year was in Miami. I was eligible for Rookie of the Year award but fell short. My failures became learning opportunities for me. I tend to relate things to sports and thought to myself, "What makes Michael Jordan great?" His natural talent made him great but his practice regimen made him an icon. I started practicing, role playing, putting in the extra hours, worked weekends, and went all in. By the end of the year, I was in Chicago for the awards banquet and all I knew was that I was in the top ten representatives in the country. My hard work payed off, my salary jumped, and now one of the pivotal moments in my life. The countdown began for the top ten. Ten was called, not me, nine, not me, five, not me, and now there were two people left. I was one of them…Boom! I was the top representative in the whole country! I did it.

I could not believe that hard work does pay off. I wanted to share the news with my parents, so I stepped outside and gave them a ring. My father, typical in his nature, blew it off, while my mother, lectured me about drinking and asked when I was coming for a visit. By now, I was used to my father not congratulating me on my life accomplishments, I think it was his upbringing but some days were rough for me. A son always wants to make his father proud and hear his father say those magical words. One day!

After being top representative in the company, I did it again the following year and then I was bored. I needed a challenge. I tried to get into management but never got promoted. I felt disrespected and left for a better opportunity. I was renting my condo out in Florida and bought a townhouse in Atlanta. After a year on the job, I became a Director for my new company. I was in heaven. I was making six figures plus stock options, bought a BMW roadster like James Bond and was living life. I still put back a percent of my check in savings. I still saved money and was on my way to accomplish other life goals.

I remember calling my dad one day and explained my frustrations with him about not being promoted. I wanted to move up in the company but some force kept denying me. His words of advice were pretty simple. Why are you trying to make a company money, when you can come home and make your family money? Basically, why I was making someone else money when I could be putting the same effort and I make money for myself. For some reason, that clicked in my head and I was on the move back home. I left Atlanta in 2008 and moved back to Florida but had to make one quick stop.

The twins and me in the house where my Dad was raised

India

Here's a thought, after completing high school, everyone should either join the military and or volunteer to go to a third world country. Before the move back home, I decided to go to India. My mother and sister from Kentucky were already there and they convinced me to come for three weeks. What a humbling experience! I took for granted the many benefits we have in America. It seems we are ruled by money here. I know we need money but somewhere along the journey we lost our way. When I arrived there, my cousin brother picked me up from the airport, along the way all I saw were tarps on the road. Tarp after tarp people were living on the side on the road.

I stayed in the house where my father grew up, which was pretty surreal. All of the modern comforts we have here in America are not common in India. For example, a modern toilet and shower system, clean water, air conditioning, internet, and paved roads. All the streets were full of different animals! We went on a trip to see a temple and on the way we stopped at a restaurant. My luck, I had to use the bathroom. Of course, they did not have any restrooms there and the owner said to go out back. There was a big rock that profusely smelled of old urine - that was a no for me. Plus I had more serious business to take care off. I was directed to go further until I saw a hole in the ground with water running and relieve my business there. I came back and my mother was laughing and asked if everything was alright. She said it is common in India to go to the bathroom in a hole and wipe yourself off with the running water. I almost did, but around the hole were spots where a few people missed the target and I just could bring myself to do it. So I squeezed my butt cheeks until we found a hotel. Spoiled much?

Probably the most humbling experience I had was at my father's house. There was a family that stayed there in the shed. They were to watch the house when nobody occupied it. This family consisted of a husband, wife, five year girl, three old boy, father-in-law and a baby on the way. They all stayed in a shed, literally. At night after the husband came home from work, they pulled out a cooker and made dinner. They did not speak a lick of English. During the day, the kids played around the property, my mother asked why the girl was not in school. They could not afford the school uniform, so my mother bought three school uniforms for her and made sure she got enrolled.

One day, I was hanging out and saw the family. I wanted to take a picture of them. As I got them closer to together and snapped the photo, the boy freaked out. They never had seen a camera before or any other electronic devices. I went and got the picture and put it in a frame to give to them. They had a look of shock on their face, I asked my mother why and she said they never seen a picture of themselves. What? They never knew what they looked like? Wow, I was shocked and in that moment I realized how spoiled I was. I realized how selfish I became when I moved to Atlanta. I missed out on a lot of family events, holidays, and birthdays. India gave me the opportunity to see where my parents came from, to see the culture. Although most people think it's a third world country, in some ways they are more advanced than we are. It's time to go home! It's time to get grounded again. Family first!

That look! I cry every time...

Regrets

I did not think I had any regrets in life. I always believed in learning from my mistakes and failure was the best teacher. However, one day my nephew asked if I had any regrets and I could not help but think of one thing. As I left home for Atlanta, I wanted to make it on my own. I wanted to be my own man. I accomplished the goals I set before me but I sacrificed other things in life.

I was so focused on succeeding and I was consumed with making my parents proud, I lost a key value, balance. I did not go home for the holidays, forgot birthdays and lost sight of family first. I remember my Mami had some event planned and I was supposed to drive an hour or so to visit but I did not make it. She asked my mother if I was the President or something. That hit home for me. No matter where I am, or who I am, family comes first.

I regret not seeing my nieces and nephews grow from children to young adults. I am truly sorry for that. I cannot take it back, but I learned from it. I will do what I can to be in their lives today. I regret having my parents work all those long hours at the store, as well as my brother-in-law. So I came home and I have not looked back. Corporate America can be grueling. It can suck the life out of you and not think twice about you. Again, you have to have balance in life. So, it's 2008 and I picked the perfect time to get grounded. The housing crisis started and I was looking to sell a home in Atlanta and buy a home in Port St. John. I needed to work on my next goal in life, finance.

My father and his brothers

Finance

I watched my father in agony back in 1987, it was called
Black Monday. My father also put a percentage of his pay
away and decided to invest this percentage in the stock
market. Everyone wants to hit the lottery, right? Black
Monday was when the stock market dropped 22% in one
day. For some it was the end of the world, for me, I was
oblivious at the time. In college I read a book by Jack
Welch, the CEO of GE and he said that was the best time to
buy. He bought banks, properties, and other assets that
propelled GE to become the largest corporation in the
world.

In middle school, one of my teachers made us play the
stock market game. She gave us fake money to invest and
whoever made the most won. I won and ever since then I
was infatuated with the market. When I turned eighteen, I
invested $1000 dollars that I saved up in the Boston
Celtics. They gave an 8% interest rate which I reinvested in

the company. By the time I was out of college the money grew to nearly $3000.

See, anyone can do that save money and invest in your future. Have patience for the market to work and set goals. After college, I sold that stock and invested in Dell Computers. It's almost like an addiction. You can make money in the market but you cannot be afraid to take risks. From there I had yearly goals that I wanted to reach in order to be able to retire early. I wanted to increase my new worth twenty percent every year, if I could achieve that, I would not have to rely on government aid when I became older. I started taking control of my money and would pay attention to trends and do my research. Remember it's your money, whether you put money in a savings account, 401K, Roth IRA, or brokerage account. It's your money!

When the housing crisis hit in 2008, I had just sold my townhouse in Atlanta and I remembered what Jack Welch said. When the stock market crashes and there is doom and despair, it's time to buy. That's how the rich get richer.

Rich people will buy stocks, property, and other assets when the price is low and sell them back to you when the price is high. So, I went with that theory and started buying stocks with the money I made on the house. I also went into the full savings mode that I learned from my mother. Every penny helped. I used coupons, turned the AC off and used a fan, never went out to eat, drove minimally, and did many other things to save a penny.

Finance is not hard; it's a choice we make. Do I sacrifice now for later? Most people live in the now and do not plan for their future. I learned how to balance the two. I can enjoy my life now but save for my future. You can too! Plan your work and work your plan.

My cousins from South Carolina, my nieces from my eldest cousin and my best friend

Choices

Life keeps moving, Father Time is consistent, and we are all in this beautiful planet for a short time. My parents are 84 and 83 today, still going strong. They still have that old school mentality and save money or haggle on a price every chance they can get. They also give back. They donate to a variety of reputable charities, sponsor causes and just help community members. This is probably the last lesson in life I have learned from them. There is always someone less fortunate than you and you can always help that person in your own way.

Life is full of choices and my family's destiny was made by some key decisions. First, my parents' choice to leave India and come to America; a decision that has had a ripple effect and impacted so many lives. They made a choice to better their lives and their children's lives. With my parents here, they influenced countless other family members. His brother in North Carolina has become a successful business entrepreneur. His two sons were afforded a great life, learning from their father. They both have children and will pass down their legacy. My father's sister is in North Florida and has raised their daughter to become a doctor. My other uncle unfortunately lost his battle with alcoholism and soon after my cousin brother lost the same battle. He left this Earth with a wife and a handsome young son. My cousin sister is married with two beautiful children and they both have great careers. My father's oldest sister never left India and has passed away. His step sister has also passed but raised three great boys. My father's step brother is in America and his son has a great career in the IT field.

My Mami is still holding down South Carolina, strong as ever! My three cousin brothers all are a success in their fields with beautiful wives and children. They all made choices. A choice to leave their comfort zone for a chance to have better lives for their children.

My two sisters' and brother in laws have a son and daughter each. All of them are having success in their life.

They raised great kids! My brother-in-laws made choices as well; they left their families to come to a new family in America. Both of are successful in life.

My parents' one choice in life led to other decisions that have changed the paths of many. As for me, I am so grateful for my parents; they are my heroes'. I have been blessed with a great life, a great family, and a great community.

A few years ago, my parents finally retired. My father enjoys gardening and annoying my mother. My mother still the lioness, enjoys cooking for everyone and has finally slowed down. We purchased the property where our store is a few years ago. The plan was to sell the store and maintain the property. Today, my-brother-law and I manage the commercial property we own.

My first dog…Bombay!

Assimilate

Every first or second generation immigrant family has to adapt to the customs in America. Most Americans do not realize how hard it is for someone to uproot from one country to another. Our country is a melting pot but that does not mean people understand the difficulty of assimilating. I think it is beautiful, how we have so many different cultures and traditions. My parents had to assimilate when they came to America. Americans could not pronounce their name, so they gave themselves an American name. Why? They did not want to ruffle feathers and just wanted to be included. Today, this is less prevalent.

We also started celebrating American holidays and traditions. My parents were not Christians but recognized Christmas. Some years we would exchange gifts with each other or friends. They also let me go out for Halloween, having no idea what that was about. We also started celebrating New Year's, Thanksgiving, and birthdays. Now, I'm not talking the lavish details some people do here but they wanted us to feel a part of the traditions in America. My parents also made sure we knew and celebrated Indian holidays and traditions.

My parents also had to learn the English language. They did not talk about religion with coworkers or neighbors. They had to let me become non vegetarian so I could eat school lunches. They let me have a pet fish. They did a great job with their children and now grandchildren. Today, we celebrate more American traditions than Indian. We are marrying outside the Indian race. We wear Nike shoes at five years old. Sometimes my parents have a hard time with the decisions we make but they know when they moved to America, and assimilation would happen.

I am very thankful they had the foresight to let their children make certain decisions on their own.

Dinner with the family in Dominican Republic

Conclusion

Today, we live in troubled times, so it seems. Our country is conflicted about many things, including racism. I always wondered why, when you're born in America, the first thing they do is label your race. When you take a test in school, apply for a driver's license, fill out healthcare forms, and a variety of other things, you have to mark down a race. Why? What does it prove? The question is, what is it creating? My whole family has dealt with racism in one form or another and by all races. We never used it as an excuse not to succeed. In general, I think America has lost some its family values and focused on a "me" society. Family first! See, with a strong family, values, education, and religion, money will come along. Does being the richest person in the world, with no family or friends make you better?

We need to get our values back! Treat everyone with kindness, love and compassion. Challenge yourself daily to become a better person. An ounce of practice is better than a ton of theory.

Be determined to succeed in life. Set goals! Be able to listen to others and learn from them. Care about your reputation and respect other people. None of these are impossible tasks; we all have it within us. Look at it like a ladder. The first step is the bottom of the rung; the top is where you want to be. Now you cannot get from the bottom to the top in one step. So, take it one step at a time and celebrate your successes along the way.

In closing, I hope this little short story can help one person out. My life now is dedicated to help others become successful, and that is not only measured by wealth. I do understand money is needed, but if you have balance in your life, you can have both.

My family took that 78 cents and made their dream into reality. We are so grateful for the family and friends we have, so grateful for what this country has given us, and so grateful for each blessing we have received along the way. I hope my family accepts this book with an open mind. Hopefully, one day, I will hear these precious words, "I'm proud of you son."

Made in the USA
Columbia, SC
24 October 2020